## Aliens Hatred

Sitting in bed
I know now I have a soul
What kind of soul
Perhaps just a voice
But something connects to that
Bids me write
Late at night
"where for art thou Juliet"
Art for thou

The lines will trip into a little bit longer
Never to the waters blood or the deserts hunger
Time to say a few words of companions spirit
And yet to talk of third moons merit
To a spinning thing of itself a unitotality
If you like not what you hear skip eternity
Be the mocking everyday shit
And go like I do to gods tender tit
Squirting and tattling all of the secrets
Well fed and bloated aliens lovers hatred

## A Huge Work

Betting on the sound of Bach
Betting on a poets lot, cold rock
Meditate confiscate enumerate
Pulsating stars surround the upward waves

Shores of up and down
Relatively standing
Asked by my son
If I passed through the earth
Would I be upside down on the bottom
Only relative to the other side
I said we wouldn't survive
Passing through the core
Then I stopped and asked
Later in time
While writing this poem
Will I embark on more words
A third book?
Haven't named the second one yet.
How will I use all my education
Staring at forgetfulness
Just letting the music entertain
Now sick how insane just entertained
I would like to be profound
I would like to live
But all are dyers all are livers
Profused by alcoholic shivers
Giving up the drink
Paint dried into my sink
And writing for the muse
Or rather from the muse
Amused
Enthused
Corporate ninja hippy shoes

## Thus Ended

Game set
Match
Really
The doing of the good
The time given you
Before the next intoxication
I cried the whole weekend
Bang bang
Am I playing a game
I doubt my love all the time
But sometimes I feel
With all the universe


## Remnants

The last remnants of our love
Did it ever exist
You wait or do not
I wait
Why
Uma kills em all
Those revenges
All dead.
Get your sword
Kill Bill

Cascade

Falling down piano up, up and on high
Note to re
To do me
The water on the lake
Only one water only one lake
Mistake
The rhyming brain breaks
Too concrete perhaps
Peach schnapps


F Underside

How could you leave me
The fields of sorrow
Left to an old cold embrace
Listening to my paranoia
All talking yet none
You can have your hell
Me mine
The piano plays I flay
To kill all of you
Broken souls your hate

Built me mine
No entrance
No love to light
Your ways
Me mine
So there
Anywhere
So then
After
Your years goodbye


Manipulating the Weather

The sky rains hope
The garden sewn dope
To grow a little high
Happy without a lie
To laugh at the distance
The pile of zucchini dirt
To grow tomatoes
To grow peaches
To grow cherrys
Apples and leaches
All have a purpose all a reason
Spinoza substance the modes a season
As the universe turns as it spins
Gravity wins pulls us all taught
At misconception

Old trees rot
Wisdom in numbers in permutations
Painting by creation
Painting by slumbers
Sleeping through the abyss
People who keep your art
They see something to not part
With
A new line in time something not seen
Before
Poetry in competence and war
To kill the night to bring
Ignorance to light
What is true?
What is right?
I ask you a question
A concept forms
Yet my ignorance deforms


Teaching the Past

Learning by writing to see
The selfsame resonance
To flee from the skys heights
The tower still fights
We are in a world of contradiction
Malfeasance and malediction
I write to compromise

To practice the pragmatics
Things can fall things can call
To Caterpillar becomings in my mind
Furry creature walks with many legs
Asking for oeuvres works
Things that beg
For our attention
People lost in conversation
What do they mean?
When they say
That was obscene
It exists things (they) that are bad
But what of evil
Has it been accepted as mad?
The distance between reason and psychosis
Is that evil
A privation
A lack when there is escalation
Can the world survive
Yes
People will come together
Organization beyond simple order
Order is not simple
It permeates everything it is determined
We fall into line at the whip
An old analogy
An old trip.

The Worlds Undertaking

The weight of my new ring
Alphabetic standards
Freedoms granite
My granny
My mom
Somewhere beyond?
My dad I love so
To face life with courage
To enrage at oblivion
To enlarge the dominion
To make our power light cracker preserved
To balance the counterpoint
Of the absurd
Is life absurd?
Contingent or pacified
Friends confide
The challenge and do wit
Can you part with it?
To work and make money
A sign of hope
Food in the fridge
Soap on a rope
New cleansers
For dirty countertops and floors
To evolve to spring
And aeons reflection
In the king

He governs a little sphere
But great deeds done by man
The king can
When the queen dies
Here is a complicated man.


The Trees of Avalon

I walk with my fishing pole
My camper
My role
I love you with words
I cannot express
You make me my wife
My empress
We fish we find
In summer heat
In summer three
The doors of perception
The sense of the sublime
I fear at beauty
I fear at love
Looking above
I wander the gailed master dwelling spelling
The universe is always telling

My pen must write my mind still fights
Stick to your guns
With nothing to shoot blue harvest compute
The severing of ties the breaking of lies
On the oil shory the owl snores
Because you left in such a hurry
To find answers to questions and glory
Do you look down from above?
No longer any hearing
Is above outside
Is below the source
The universe believes of course
I ask my humble insight
To see a little
In tree form life
Aborescent rhysomatic dance.


Leverworld

A place where you can extend your energy
A hardcopy entropy
Disassembling reassembling
Not what you create
But what you do not destroy
How to make money for chatter
Before the morning clatter
Foraging foliage foremost
A piece of toast

Bread they said
Would make you sick
Dairy also quick
I knew her once
Thought I might love her
But I guess I didn't
Nice girl interesting
Never a dull moment
Passages and friends
To reconnect and make all right
Leave her
Leverworld


Esther at the Bottom

To invoke you I did not really intent
Back to the crusted sun listening
Concrete glistening rhythm
To propose her man wiggles
Her toes
Esther you are free again
Love came to your door...Friendship for ever more


The Whole World is Watching

Deep space synthesizer
Bellowing gates upward the storm

The meteor pierces the ring
And enters a trajectory unsatisfactorily
The moon dust up up up into deoxygenated air
The chemist boils his last concoction
The alchemist prays to his benefactor
Science has revealed but faith
Faith in the past- does it exist anymore
Are all trajectories realized in time?
A line a lake ripples pond scum
Morning dew
The slug of appetites crawls up the blade
Just a small slug
But just any slug will do
The pen dries I need two.


Whold Watching

Creepstare death beware
Crawling from the slime
Bacterial crime
To take your biology
Left only to little fear
To make men care
To watch the truth
Love renewed
Polypeptides
Ontological rides
In a park

Amusement
Won


A Prayer

As our earth so beautiful
So fragile perhaps not
The balance that sustains humanity
Is probably the fragility
In a few years all our creations
All our misgivings would be covered
If I was one of the last fragments
That survives what should I leave
How to welcome space and time
The miracle of food
The miracle of life
Stainless steel seems the better bet
Don't sweat I'm not god
God wouldn't wipe it all away
Fighting for my hope
Striving for my sanity
Against a formidable enlightenment
Spelling always calls
Looking to rhyme in hallowed halls
The people look and desire
While the leaders go to the wire
Telephones one
Star trek metaphysics

Is it possible that justice
Survives to the future
How is that for advanced technology
Thinking on the page
No longer a rage
A prayer at noonday sun
Looking for the one
Coffee just called but I'm up
At night
For a cup.


More Illity

Ill at tea in the lime sun afternoon
Love breaks open the piñata
Candy falls to the ground
More illness to believe in love
Make the words beautiful the poems hopeful
Morality beacons from the sublime
Infected with light darkness runs
To the evil night doctor
Voodoo exchanges love rearranges
And all is well again
Thinking of the carribbeans
How to spell?
Too lazy to look it up
I could keep writing the word
Until one looks right

Spelling with my head speller


## Head Speller

Caterpillar yellow black
Climbs to Corner Brook leaves
The backyard I was a child who
Knew some of nature
I cannot walk away from life
There is too much invested
In this universe
My entrapment my endearment
My love will live
Bringing hate a popsickle
Bringing hate some bread
Bring love all those things
And a new bed.


## Words So Wonderful

The royals have arrived
To see our little world
Separate from the whole
A little hole
People so naive
They will hate at my reprieve
Little rhymes
Yet many good times

The music in my background
Dracula a little from the heart
Blood bled to depart
So every lonely in travesty
They will never love
No ever no ever lived
Words so wonderful
Time gived


Time Given

All the hopes striven
The fly on the bespectacled barrens
And love so ready
To put yourself in the cyber sea
To find live love family
The time has come
When purgatory became
To give up the sins of the past
Atheist wanderings
There is no god
So say the brights
Sirens in the background
Ambulances of nights


Supernatural Banality

Profane is the darkness

The light a lie
To give hope
When hope wants to die
The love of the eternal
A consequence of relativity?
To understand rationality
Ask me I know
I know madness
I know people
Venal capitulary
Unforgiving
Contrary
Betting on the long shot
Hating the truth
The truth keeps me scarred
And keeps me forsooth
I look to piano
Madness the instrument
Of empires
To sit in audience
Of vampires
Sucking eating no
They draw blood when eating
Your dearest desires
To live forever
I suck your intent
Out of your mindsphere
To repeat
To yourself

All the dreams you have had
Supernatural banality
And forgiveness sad.


Happenstance Has Married

To know
That you have found joy
Makes me happy
My decision
To leave you
For the better
My boy
I thank you
With all my heart
That we have a son


Poesis By Summer Sweat

I contrive to find
In firey summers mind
The scope of intent
Preserving the freedom
Of the present
Marble churches
Could not find
The rhyme times
To scratch to make

Concepts for the take
We read
We talk
We find
We walk
The pressure
Of making
The worlds undertaking


What God I Lacked

Going without to remember
"ancient Gods they watch and listen"
Never there
Just our little planet
Without hope
That is real
Living for today
Saying yes to life
No to the eternal lie
I lived to you
My poetry in bad faith
Science is our best friend
Culture will also mend
Don't stifle the free thought
Let criticism wash you
Let your peers judge you
Leaving the lost

Believing in the human host
Gathering not deceiving
What can I tell you
Will you follow me
For the short time
I have on this planet
This is the answer I have
Been waiting for
No god
Just humans who think
They are gods
Fighting internecine wars
Tribulation for leaving
Our besting chores
Still more poems to come
Yet food yet rum.


Diotima

She teaches love and beauty
She teaches together forever
She teaches true sight
She lasted in the weather
She passed on through our night
What makes it all worthwhile
Is where we spend time together


Toys Of an Atheist

Left handed nation
How I became an atheist
Facing death
Believe it is real
Stupid religion
Where will come
The satisfying meal?

Toying with an art
Of the future
No god no devil
Only human suture
Snapping at the meek
Screaming at the mild
Everything is going wild

Create something
Just words in transit
Listen to the music
If you can stand it
Those who have lasted
Those who never fasted


Demiurge

Setting the universe going
All the fields and forms
Stepping back to have it

Permutate into creation
Perhaps you had no choice
Perhaps there is no voice
To listen to all the screams
My mind and truths seams
Holding together all the sights
Perhaps it was all designed
By a fiend
Or was it all accident
On through the chilling night
We humans must make
The maelstrom home
We must build like Rome
On the rubble of the past
Civilizations
To rule with wisdom
Love and understanding
The only way to make it all
Worthwhile
The past like the Nile
Flooding its banks
To feed the plants
For food and hope
Perhaps it was all planned
Unlike this role
Equipped to everlast
Remembering the past
Beyond we go
For ever more.

## To Love The God

God seems to be everywhere
The Necker cube perception
No god needed for love
No hope needed just the peace dove
To bond together in some way
Of togetherness
Through the night of unhappiness
To rise in the morning and volunteer
Your souls for love and understanding
The metaphysics of the universe
Can switch the cube
And all you see is accident
The universe round and bent


## Yonder

Now I am beyond her
I tried to love
When it wasn't real
Once again I can feel

I lived in lost jealousy
The temple of hope sanctity
We are all in this together

My lands temperate weather

We feel fog and mist
We feel sleet and rain
I feel normal now
No longer insane

The hope this brings to me
To a world that sometimes goes mad
Is that with care and sobriety
We can learn to live
Live consciously

Yet when it all seems to much
A little drug a little touch
Some rum some beer
Forgetting about the fear

Some get madly drunk
And reach out with their fists
The sublime covers the innocent
In the laws goods insist


Normocarn

The normal in their carnival
Ipod this Ipad that

Computer souled
Nothing meant

Nothing meant
Nothing felt
Still something
Bitter nothing

As the stars the sun the moon
I travel at knighted way
Looking for good
Looking for play

I sat thinking one day
With my pen in hand
My a brain a legal point
Just sand

Crispy wind and fires rose
All around me
Deathly repose
I sat in hell that time
Felt the world was something
Sublime

Will you follow me
The razors edge
Between good and bad
Still strangely sad
Could this be hell?

No knowing (Not well) feeling well?


Lost on The Level

I creep into deathless stares
My soul might be lost unawares
I smile into deaths homely grip
My mind in writing begins to slip

I came to this light out of endings
Beginning seems to me to be sending
What I lost on a past meant that
I could become what happening spat

Out of the spheres
Of lonely worlds
The young beacon
To the old seeking

I creep into deathless stares
Your fiction makes me aware
Of possible worlds calling
Our loves being taken in the walling


Higher Found

I once was found too high
I could not resist the feeling

And now I am seeing
What the new drug does
To our children
They are lost but they see something
What do they see
Other being transtemporality?
We in a sea of universes
Yet a set of sets
Members of themselves
Members of nothing
Diotima what was your call?
I sit and smoke
For what else does a lonely god do?
I seek to understand
Do I?
Do I love you? My reader?
Love is so grand a thing
I wax at waxing
And I wane when there is an ending
To give when all I want to do is take
What can I give?
Money…that's my responsibility
The insects at night
Fly all over Europe and they eat
All the foliage
Yet we party and drink when we can
Where does it all lead to
Heaven?
Why put us all through hell

You might as well
Because you are lonely too.


Heat

The heat of my resurrection
Sweet trances of confection
To taste and tamper
With my passive candour
Action in contemplation
The heat of the world
The sounds unfurrelled
A bet sitters dream
The light a beam
To stay and feel
While the worlds slaves kneel
The boundaries of the scarlet stars
Blood
Hampering the misogynous fevers
To anthropormorphize my style
The god endeavours
The God's new 'clevers'
They talk and beam
While the counterfeit seams pull
Together the cooling cloth
Together the mothball hawks
Sitting to hunt
Sitting to walk

Walking mile of seven hells bells
Learning to feed on the other side
Of their brains
You read me
Thanks you make it all possible
My heat and the sculptors crucible
Casting a weathered glow
In the night of caspers
Friendliness
A pompous measure if ever my pleasure
For things dead and gone.


Ask

When I ask myself
What do you have to say?
I see prose neglected
For poetries way
I look for inspiration
I know it comes from work
Me new job seems so simply
As clerk
Assisting others in their struggles
For meaning
Can I enter such a task
To learn all you need
Is to ask.

## Dark Ocean

In the myrth of my darkness
I appeal to your weakness
For my pity
Pity of me
Sitting to write
A greatest of gifts
Spend thrift with my words
To connect with those who would read
No longer a slave free to be
Free
Some time on my hands
I must spend it wisely
I have music for my soul
To never cajole
The beauties line
Mine in the sublime
Contemplation


## Believe Me

Girl
I cried so many tears
The thunder of all those

Years
Another calls?
Maybe?


Winter Eyes

Can you see me there
Out in the courtyard
The snow falls
Like our love?
A documentary
To wait
To see
Alpha male?
Alpha girl
Maybe?
Possibly maybe?
Life lives
And gives strength
Biologist.
Pickles? Haha!
Don't you know
How I feel
Seventies goodbye
Goodbye
My love.
Music!
The pain!

Phobos

A moon by any standards
Yet secrets
And calling
Out into deep space
The displace
Of all our contents
Scream at life
Scream at death
Phobos you've met
All music
All calls
The sleep the dreams
And the sing
Be pure be free
If that could be me
Be me.
I've waited for your call
Did you wait for mine
Phobos the entente
Of our entreaties
To wait to list
To the spheres
Divine madness
I have seen

Have you?
I have seen.


Involved Opiate

Can you hear me out in the cold
Can you feel me before I'm sold
Planets revolve and hate circumscribes
The letters the jibs and jives
The matter evolves the stars crumble
Porceline universe so bold
Cracks in the vector the stars
The skys the hope the danger
Pulls drawn the involved opiate


Do You Starlight, Love Me?

You came from far far away
Do I need your love today I bless becoming
Change and the chain rattles I have qualities
Few can imagine I'm subtle
Few subtle and few rebuttle
I feel humbled but stars blast out of my eyes
'Darkness breeds anarchy'
Future bearer seeping " logic fleeting"
Bleeding loneliness in solitude
A state of mind together
I am judging you now

What are you to me?
You don't read my work to see
You are connected to nothing
The lies the weak sow
Fields of regrets and moons of iron
Rusting in the neutrino soup
Radioactive sex lights the day
Brighter than chrysalis suns
Can we bring the hate together
To create?


Underground, a Parabola

A parabola curves our intent
To see you judged to add to
The hate escaping into truth
Drinking the poison to feel the zone
Zeniths of distant points
Over the horizon of our malnourishment
To leave if there is any time left
To contact the living, the dead
Our pride instead
The love I once knew
The buttons and the beeps to connect
You cannot see I cannot see
Don't tell me you know for we are madness
Madness and the bleeps of us

Entrapment I can feel the spheres
Holy motions deft years
To breed the state of triumph
Willing, feeling, caring, lots of death
Lots of life I avoid challenging you
I can break myself, perhaps you
But I choose not to lengthen
Your life and burning
Underground a parabola
Bent circumscribing a malnourishment
Over the horizon as the stars
Burst out of my eyes
I am saved and lost
I feel the cost as alone again
I suck my intent up into
A horrible singularity
I call a mind a hope
Entrapment of enfeeblement
The horizon and underground, parabola, is


Hopefully I Win

Anamnesis I wager
To the polychromius evil
As the splice entreats my trna
Invoking the speciality of effect
A dead man talking
The meno slave ,remember what was told

But forgets what was once learned
The empty church and love lost
Owner of a lonely heart
Much better than an owner of a broken heart
Stolen first born , intent
And her regret
Too proud to be a believer
Too proud a pure deceiver
Cannot face the temptation
As apples kernel caresses
The fly born bespectacled garden
Growing hopes and lies
And loneliness devours my last love
All I feel are rivers washing
Rivers drowning the seas of all eyes
My stage fright my intent
Drank to a stupor I still write
To hope to light my ways
To decide on hopeful beginnings
And healthy strivings
To bleed blood to bleed love
To give to decide her eyes
So callous so empty
She does not see and my dreams
They forgot the swollen seems
Functionally illogical irrelevance
To forget happenstance.

## My Lady New

Blossoms blooming in June sunshine
To stay strong to be good
Being good  being hopeful
I must remember all the good you bring
My lady you help me create how I feel
Here on this page my words
Borrowed from a great hope a great star
Feeding all the universe
Compatibilist?
Try to keep us friends
Of the best kind
The trees murmur with the wind
The sea frolics
I miss you when you are not around


## Compare Here

I like to love looking at
To believe in blessed truths
A post human entreatment
To live as a god
Amongst the wreckage
I look to love as the stars
Rise and fall, all the hope
For her love I pray
But to what an order

A flux to secret the cabin
In a country shore
Believe in me
You can set me free
I've invested in you
The trees the hills the creamy cows
Push em over topple
The ivory tower becomes
And a gun to my head
Do it! do it! now!
"But that was just a dream"
I awake to post crisis
Summonings and I learn
It all unwravells in merit
Merit for sanguinary hope
For trepadacious act
Calling searching to express
In a poem a heat soup
Stirring in star sea
Abyss heaven and a mass
The sight the light
And I pause for secrets.


Her Thumbs

Her thumbs I remember
Like Fiona apple
She was supple

Bona fide
Beautiful
I am free to write again
I could not live the lie
But good things can come from bad
But look at what I lost
Are you willing to pay the cost
If you have found her
Cherish her she is the one
"the sun will come out"
"just saying it can even make it happen"
Goodbye thumbs.


Knowing Your Love

A beginning everyday
The sun shines the beautiful way
Energy and hope the comfort
Of knowing your love
Doubts leave me
Hope be me
I do appreciate you
I need you, I want you
The chemicals mix
The day wants and bleeds
Water; bloods hope
Pass the rope
I'll pull us together

Through summer storms
The heat informs
And leaves me wise
For a while and then the loss
To live again, your mind
My friend
The other no other


Falling From Grace

What is grace?
Technology?
Falling into nature
Staring into hell
Salvaging the last hope of humanity
The principle
They will say it exists
Think positive
Look to the past
The piles of hate
Of bones.


God & The Devil

Does anyone see like I see?
God created the devil
God creates reality
In human terms we need friendship

Loneliness tears us away from the light
Is god alone with no equal
Only the creation before the eyes
Our father lives in a nightmare
Or are there other omnipotent gods
To keep company
Perhaps the devil recognized the loneliness
Of god and rebelled
To fight as a part against the other
To keep deities memory and hope
God alone so alone
Creation and knowledge separate?
These are mysteries I cannot answer at this time.


Humans in Hell

Every human passion denied
All love full of lies
All truth illusion
All hope confusion

All light all see
The hate of eternity
The dark secret
Eternity time

Thyme and Rosemarys
Baby
To be scared to death

An escape
Perhaps to better

Madness and eternal solitude
Save the love save the hope
Gods memory failsafe
Forgot about his son?

Crucified, embalmed, alive
The past yet the future
My madness something
Made in replete silence

Starving and burning
Insects eating worms burroughing
Through my feet
And rice and grain
Is a feast to eat


Gods People Rage

They see what is wrong
For how long?
Till pillar topping poppers
Of pills tell
All the lies that subdue
"but never tame us"
For the shame of us
Music must live

We will conquer
Rise above live to love
Gods people rage
Rage for the last strands
Of humanity


Metal Is Dead?

The rage of right
The rage of safe keepings
The darkness of the night
The grim harvests reapings
To bring into the light
The further future bearers seepings

Merciful Fate

To think the devil would hold
A special place of pleasure
For me in hell
At the side of truth
The side of righteous hope
To keep God alive
Or is the devil a rebellious fool
Taking human love and dashing
It upon the rocks
It upon the docks
Ships from long journeys
The bible only part of the plan

And us left only with man.


The Impinetive

The rascal hapless smudge
The deep bloodge clots trudge
Onward into the future of blood
The deep roosters broods
The words when sober
The diamonds fate
The charge, the church
Of holy others
Hoping for life
The stoic love
To bear the given
To become the striven
Striving to life
To hope


Friends of the Devil

At the right side of god
The infinite human mysteries
To become wise
To know the love, the sacrifice
The freedom of our political system
Allows us to reconnect to the ancient

Systems of truth
The connection
A resurrection
Left alone to write
But connected
Strong, alive becoming




When I Awake

Will I see my words as appropriate
Life must grasp the hope
The world a place of mystery
Can you last
Can you cope
The fist of the misery




Drunken Reprieve

Apocalypse now
I scream for the end
But why?
"its all so beautiful
To me"
Why?
"I don't want to change the world
I don't want the world to change me"

"to break new ground of a new frontier"
"frosty the snowman"
Drunken bliss
Hapless happenstance


One Time

Celebrating our differences
Consolidating our differences
Respecting our differences
To have a sense of our transcendent oneness
We are all linked somehow
Déjà vu insight, remembering dreams
That is all it is
Remembered dreams
Keep your dreams, act by them
Set the worthy goal
For your worthy soul


Creation

An act, the only one, believe
Don't believe you don't even have to care
Our mortal breaking souls


War

A fog I cannot see my way
The paths are hidden
And death the only day
My child and his mortal bones
Bespeak a tragedy lost homes
The blood bleeds out a gaping wound
And rattling tanks planes ships bound
Only the begging a demoniance
So terrifying that if you knew
Would drive you truly mad
My eyes look to the ground today
The starlight has fallen in the night
No hope to believe in no sights unbound
The slavish pen cannot make what it is
And sorrow so profound
A duty calls my rational mind
Mutually assured destruction
Forces poised or at least prepared
To stave off violent illnesses
And quake with Everest sound
So high so lofty our human hopes
When my family is gone will I dangle
Upon a choke rope?
No I must carry on must stay the mist
Believe in love
I won't be lost in tryst.


Sins

Staring into the lonely night
What do I see, the face of eternity?
To covet mothers bride
Mine is out there somewhere
A universe of purpose
A memory of a face
Do not go there
The latest obsession
And love withdraws
Am I ready for love
No.
Do I want love?
I don't know
I do yes
That was yesterday
And tonight
Maybe dreams and visions
Feeling the one
Knowing and striving
Hope must live must embrace
It always has for me
So I pass on not my sins
But my grins.


Only the Brave Survive

Only the instance of kind
The movie rewinds
Of my life
And a living of another
Grammar cannot escape
I claim I escape
The rhyme returned
I will look for my partner
My friend of beyond.
Are you the chosen one
Am I?
Will the evil triumph
Take me down
As a sacrifice
To be eaten
By the gulls of hell.

Only the Strong Deny

I am free and strong
My hope lasts long
Life does not take me down
The intoxicating lie
The denying try
Sex the to love
To the above
Love most holy

## Across the Page the Universe I Give To You as Love

I am chemically drawn
To your passion
I feel right now
As if the whole universe
Could feel if I do
As I do
Across the page the universe
I give to you as love


## The Universe

Dare I to sit in my basement
At unfinished construction
Listening to the electronic waves crashing
Into my speakers
God flows and is angered
Smashes the plastic window wrap
Perhaps it is time for bed
Where can I bring you
To my dreams to my life eyes
Lifted ever so closed
To see into eternity?
You may feel you may think
But you cannot create
But I can
Not the words chosen to hear

Time to drink.


Alone 3

Picking the momery off the pile
The throne melts, always free
To find another, to smarten the whip
Neglected duties and relapse
To free the ghosts of my entente
Measure escaping meaning, the subconscious hides
Many miles many roads, star paths
Star paths and displaced eros and beauty
Beauty always attracts in the universe
Does the beauty outsum the planet and its ugly
Or is all of it good?
Depends on your perspective
God's eyes? All around "sound fury and lights"
Tragedy does it get to knock on the door
Or is triumph all we need?


The Outer Threat

Inner space, outer space, space
Places or traces can displace
The soul or personon the soul
Denumerated and dissolved, the threat?
That we are basic to greater eyes
Humanity? Ha parasites to our planet

We have arrived from the past, tou tou
Enantiomorphs

Snacks

Here I sit beer and snacks
Onion snacks and people long gone
Everybody laughed at me
I think I hate myself
Would I do it over a cliff
I do, I hate myself
A gift from God wasted
Yet why am I here
Just to end it?




Girls and Women

To make the transition
From cuties to cuddlys
I guess that was yesterday
Yet no woman no love
Barren horizons and pain
Complaining at my present lot
One on the horizon
Maybe she's the one
Perhaps she's the one
Maybe I'm lying to myself

Summerland

Maybe I've got it
Maybe my skys can still be blue
Maybe I'll find you
Is that the way a man is
Supposed to think


La,La,La

God I can't take it anymore
Why me why so alone
No one to call my own
Just the memory
Maybe you don't exist
What do I mean when I say
I believe in God
No one alone in around
The music so loud
Goodbye happiness.
Going mad
Going mad
How do I survive this
Goodbye
Ghost leave me alone
Leave me alone.

Hate

The H words.
A synaptic artificial
Neural nets
Stereoscopic vision
Las Vegas bets
The noise stills
The lapses and frequents
On times shore
Just the matter
The universe expands
The big bang


Words

Words must come
There must be meaning
We must not be lost
We must not be simply
Objective
But also subjective
Real vision and reaction
Contemplation of what is
What is being
Yes that's all
We need meaning

# The Dastardly Deeds Of the Devil

The dastard bastard comes
Taking intuition fruition
Apples oranges plums
Deduction destruction
Tanks planes guns
Sleepy sleepy mist
Sleepy sleepy kissed
An envelope ensued
The D pushes its way in
Ensues
Seeing the suers
Sewers of man
Omnipotence and energy
Yet yet yet
Niet dieing killing
Taking and laughing
Cigars, popes and bishops
The last vestibules of religion
Poor hope, poor love
Poor hate for what is wrong
Poor truth, poor essence
Breathing from none such
None such weather
None such
None like
All alike

Brave new world
The fear
Three types
Heidegger?
Invoking names
Is any man the devil or just a pawn.


Millennium Requiem

Goodbye to past years
Past fears
Onto new hopes
What will carry us on
All of us
Relativity
Passive gold gods listen
Tides of horizons change
Past peoples
Old ages
From space the outer tidings
Ether breathings
The end of judgement
Just the calculation remains.


Facades 2

I can withdraw into
Infinite mirrors

You will never see me again
Is that what you want?

I can withdraw into
Infinite mirrors
You will never know me again
Is that what you want?

Is anything worth having?
Is anything worth saving?
What words can you use
What entreatments can you make?

I can withdraw into
Infinite mirrors
You will never feel me again
The eyes of all the people.

It is just sad
Hopeless really
We could not get along
You were always willing
To move along
Is it that you see me  as less?
Had no faith in my love?
And even less
In a literal world
Are many contradictions
What's worth saving?

What mirror is worth smashing?
You'll never find me again.


Winter

Trudeau in the storm
Vivaldi, Mozart
True to form
Stand and be counted
The past surmounted
Vision, passion
Forlorn?
A nation stands in mourning
A lesson through peace
To see with eyes
Out of tears our duty
To the world
To surmount our fears
The guide
To smile, to think
To unite in hope
To remember a man
Who was lucky, was excellent
If more were like him
But what are we all?
What we are given?
Or what we create?
To mold our world

To mold ourselves
Or to unfold
To talk-to hear?
And most importantly
Is is courage
Is is knowledge
Bringing forth the souls
Into heaven reappear


On Being

Will I live forever
Transient, never
I have to hope
Look he hopes dumb human
The haunting in my brain
Driven insane
I wish I could be like the others
Believing in God
Still I pray
Hope to end terrors day
The final end no cause
Because I don't go on
Even so I must leave you with
Positive bandwidth
So you can look up beyond the skys
And live with stars
In your eyes

Or better yet
Your own star
And journey afar.

Red

There is more than one red
They are not derived from one red
Multiple universes, universals
Many colors but still one word, Red

Halloween

The horror we visit
Visited among us, in eyes
Upwards glancing to the skys
Ever forever, Gods entreat
The fear of downness, bottom of feet

Die Walkure

Apocalypse now or later
Before they fought, we fight
Forever but when the universe dies
Relative eternity, the blood
On everyone's hands
A splitting atom, the Cartesian theatre
Where am I?

The sound of the future, the past
The sound of silence
The plane of movement
Moving creatures forever
Oh yea I said that (forever)
What is forever? Elliptical
Rhombus, trapezoid, cars trucks
Flowing stoned ducks
Crossing muffin man roads.
Beef eating cigar smoking toads
Withdrawing from ethics, morality
Vampyrisms to steal the bodies
But the brain breaks down
Dennetts soul is subject to entropy
Listen the gold gods glisten
To Costa Rica Liberian on Ghanas Border
More murder, hot meddle what
Settles, settles mettles
Condominium, under water home
Over bones and wipes and roads.
(roads) I guess I said that too
Building, saving, the passage of energy
Energy pockets
Super creative scientist
Getting pissed
On the new drugs.


Nothing Left To Say

Nothing left to say
Saying out loud and without meaning
Do you know my secret?
Do you know the universes secret?
Ordinary madness as we hear
The power calling to all the dead
The powers of the living
 Living in contempt of court
The universes justice, the gavels of time
Bang…bang…bang!


Underthings

Underwear over worn and wholes
Parts and development free circles
Round and round the imaginary lace
And writing suffers high art
High experience
Depart.


Fungus

Primus and fungus
Pick my toes with rows of peas
Blast the gas of burning trees
To erupt a spoonful of peanut goo
To pick the gum off my shoe

To roll down hills of spiny seeds
To sit in ponds and snack on reeds
To climb a tree with ballet shoes
If you get to the top you can snooze
Jump off into a cloud and sink
Fresh jello is in the sink
And the hockey rink is pink
Pink cotton candy and wiener dogs
Rogs and mogs and hogs and fogs
Drifting in on the pebbled beach
Jelly fish and dead caplin reek
Stink stinky little fever to burn
The buckshot beaver.


Freedom to Criticize

Yea you don't step out of line
We see you, you punk!
Get a haircut dig a ditch
Your mother was a witch
Burn your lazy lazy contempt
And work and repent
Or we will nail you tooth and all
To cross. Yea you in the mall
What are you looking at?


Red Ink

Red ink and Russian roulette and think
Because the crypt call, chastises criticizes
The agent in Agatha to astronauts in august
Murdering disgust melt mesmerizes meets
They tease temp taught pulls endeavour
So very clever cleaves and castigates
Full bloom blasts being beavers bounce
Big bountiful baskets of boron
Krypton radon racoons and rotting raisins


Red Ink 2

Caustic fairers measures rolling
Spin into out consoling the red ink corrects
Abjects but listens to the future
The bringing sound the bringing round
Back to corrections to the bad
To the good to remunerate a nation
To give to truths station.


Red Ink 3

Trilogy interestedly complacently
Now I wish to reveal to everyone
My money making
The truth that cannot be born
The truth that is shared
Can I wravell up the hateful spins

To red ink the mistakes
To help who that creates
Beginnings of wisdom
The hope
And the lasting.


Words of Healing

Quiet?!
'bitches' brew
Deconstructed mate
All females or men
Quiet!
Harbinger


The Yellow Nimbus 2

Playing God again?
Or just some angel
Or my little part
Making art
The rhymes to end
But love to mend
And all I need is?
Hmm hymn babim
Scalamoosh, ashabosh.

A Farewell to a King

Saw G Lee today
On the tv
Strange. I was telling a friend
That P Trudeau was pure Canadian
Like Rush. Rather personally
I valued them both like that
I'm sure there are others like vie void
Voi Vod 'in league with the devil'
Don't get me wrong I like all those
People for what I know
Everyone's an artist
Only a few are assholes.


Closer to the Heart of Me

Hey truthfully-I like all three.


Listen To The Rain

I am listening to the recorded rain-myst
Sound so present to hear-there
I call the night binder the matter finder
Out there in here, in there, out here
I call the night binder, dark matter
I call the matter finder, out there
A machine so big so wonderous

A sonorous march to work  all look
Upward into the traces of god
A light cone a past betrayed
A building out there through here, immanence
The I of planets calling hearing
Listening to the recorded rain
Will it feed my crops, my city crop
In pull the endeavor of millions of units
The matrix influence and time spend
Down a back alley
Can I lift you up help bear your load
Together we can turn this ship around
Slow down technologies progress the negative
To build the true conservation
I am a hypocrite I have not taken measures
And hope severs , sever from the pain
Of unrealized dreams to find new ones
'dream on brothers and sisters'
"someday I'll be an honest man"


The Worker

Sitting at table bare
Wax in hand and imagination
Grand
Pulling together the ideas
He is a merchant of ideas
Wholesale

Many thoughts for hire
To bring hope and love
The worker again
A maker full to seed
Planted
To grow and need
To live and pass the expanse
Bring together a little one
Dances
The sculpture he breathes
His life into
Making art
High prices don't connect
But yet they buy
Art world
World of art
The strange, the profound
Found again
Absurd?
Love you can depend
Albedo .39
The earth captures the light
Energy alright
Again again
Nothing new
But perhaps
Peach schnapps

You Can

You can you can do it
Try harder
Try any amount
Momentum hope you can
You can
You can do it
Create mold deliver
You can, you can do it
Build, plant, harvest
Dwell you can
You can do it
Write, sing, love
You can, you can do it
Live spend, save, cure
You can, you can do it
Love, hope, faith
Yes its true
The news you can
You can do it
Fear, run, hide
You can, you can do it
Die spend again
You can you can end
But why, why preserve?
Lift up from your slumbers
Lift up from your isolation
Look around life

It is waiting watching
Love
Love can be yours
Love can give
Love is true
You can.


The Revealers

Creators destroyers
Revealers, covers of up
A cover up
An open door
To pull together
To pull apart
Is all of this-art?


When The Noble no Longer Care

When the noble no longer care
All is left unawares
The splice of past and future bare
To be led by God to the fair
We can dream
We can make
We can work for a better tomorrow
Are we noble any longer
Do we face dark masted night

On the sea of existence
Like we are there?
All expansion
Tunnelling merit to infect
The body, a temple
Stay pure stay clean
Do not foul your mouth
Speaking the obscene.


The Vastness Of Space

I am looking and I see
That which leads me
Outward, beyond, the reaching
Stars above. Stars bellow
The thunderous ruins, the ship
Into the night, sky a sky of lights
Mythodea what does that mean?
A myth that we are human
The sound of reconciliation
Sirens on wavy oceans
Wavy star system, wavy planets
We have not made contact yet
Is this the myth?
Perhaps we do have a ship
A few bodies to boot
New technologies to understand, to master
Outerspace is vast

What does Kant mean?
A-priori looking glass we bring space
And time to things in themselves
We order reality
Just remembering this bids me
To put down my pen and search
My memory does me no justice
Perhaps I never understood a thing
Philosophy is like this to me
I can read and things all seem
Barren
Unlike the universe, vast
Neverending.


Sinfonia

Phoney baloney
Sin roley poley
The world a better place
Got to be
Or all is nought
Fraught with endings
Love hope faith
Evermore embrace


Food

The world needs food for everyone

The world please put down your guns
Don't make so many children
You have choice
To live a long and prosperous
Productive life
Everybody have hope and love
Try to live by the golden rules
Kant and Christ
A universal maxim
And treat others as how you
Would be
Could be.
Goodbye

Goodbye girl
Someone holy
Someone there
Mother of my child
Yes I do care
Have a happy life
It took us apart
For me to value you
I needed someone else
Someone better for me
My sins, years
Equality calls
Love of all that lives
Love of all
Peace and happiness to you

Find true love
Find care
Find


Beacon

The deacon of the beacon
Is reekin of pecan
Subtle spring frost pie
Pumpkin death savored pie

Speaking of reekin pecan
Seeking the scent of compost rye
The still in the severed water
The mastered flim
Survival guest and scent.

Becoming under the weather
Overman superman
The love of life
Must persevere over all technology
If you must work to tend your garden
Do so do so
But all the while it must remain
Technology
But all our human art do not multiply
Seek origins seek new beginnings

Have the holy host for breakfast
Meet the God of tincture
Ointment spread bagels
And wanders nonsense.


## Consciousness & Happiness

When drink is in your veins
The yearning, the brilliance
Of anothers displace
To brink you to the bring
Of extinction
Mumbling on mumbling with
Will you see my will
Good? Bad?
Autonomy for the sad?
To bring the love of God
To consciousness
And happiness.


## God Is Good

God reveals all
In time
Gives love and sight
To recognize our gifts
I must confess
I go from a rage

To happiness
Only to find
My limited'it' mind
Keeps me doubtful
At this stage
And hope to be a sage.


Sublime Climb

The climb to the top is so hidden
Tell me that your futures not ridden
With bullets and guns and snakes and rum
But that was the old days
Now we got aids and crack
The god is dead on its back
Love is lost and forlorn
Yet it all could change
For the better
Faster fuller freer


The Cycle

Has ended suffocation
Embalmed embodiment
Into the vortex into the abyss
Down ever ending, never
The light become darkness
The souls all free

How Are You?

I am fine thank you
How are you?
So so I guess
Whats next
I wonder
You wonder
We feel and touch
Writing stopped
Part past into the zone
The sound of sadness
Don't write or read
That's my need


Fake Genius

The existentialists create themselves
I destroy myself, see here I go again
Picking up the pieces pulling up
The boot straps
Listening, hoping for inspiration
Work for the works sake
Gita, gita seniorita
Where is she now
The weather, the years of singularity
Still looking not finding
Perhaps I'm not ready for love

Something is happening
When I read through the pages
In don't see, it seems eye to eye
Yet isn't the creator just a bit high
High up, high out, deep in
Provihito in altum
To be above the precipice
The darkened hours, ticking
Switching, digitizing
To leave something
I am a father now
The joy is good, my son
 I love his times now
I love mine with him
So young so new, smiles
For everyone, I am I up for the challenge?


The Waves of Being

Outer space calls for journey long
Journey lonely, journey strong
Our efforts build at home and call for glory
Glory strong and told of past ages
The minds of many cold space culture
In awe we still can look to the stars
Those who frequent this heavenly gaze
Can still look in awe and lead us
Navigators a mind in search

To have found what we are looking for
Who has? Desire and flows , beginnings
Love still grows. Our planet may be in need
Or is it just want. If need can be fulfilled
Then we have more time for want
The fixed heavens the round earth
Those minds who challenged and brought to birth
Hidden in the latin the ancient greek
A fortress first made, made not weak
  I want to reach out for the sublime
The mystic comprehension an ego in bloom
To raise the others to rise to greatness
To understand the universe a room
To house the nurse of becoming
The cradle of the forms
The gods wait watch and listen
To the outer rings the outer spheres
Mythodea copper belts
To celebrate our friends
To yearn together perhaps power made
Power over stuff not those with
A principle of devotion
The outer stars the waves of being
The stars retrieving
Deep space scientist seeks life
Looks within completeness not found
Becoming calls to life from death
The good that which completes
Life not complete death a retreat

The stars flicker above him
A fireside beach experience
Love within reach calling outward
Calling with love begin
Memory melds the galaxies
Memory melds the tapestries
Knit into births knit into lives
The sewn the reaped the harvest
The waves of becoming wash the titles
The waves of becoming and change


Heaven

Have I drunk from the waters?
Eternal youth yet Cain
Eternal circumnavigation, the universe?
The universe


Stranger

"What lies behind my stare?"
Would you even care
What you've done to me
How you've treated me
Goodbye forever
You are only a stranger
Could never feel me
Didn't try hard enough didn't give enough

What you did to me
What I did to you
Speak anything
Speak before you fade away
Speak talk stay
Just be?
Become who you are
Speak


Cyber Poem

Aha wasting paper
Put it in my cyberspace
Hide your soul away
To be lost
In the aeons
The femtos and the nanos
Owing a piece of me
My time all the same
The beer wears off
And onion breath
Taking over


Sound

Simple sound
Sound profound
Others call and level

More strength to God
Mystic listening to God
The universe abound
Strength always comes
As long as I have the sound.


This Medication Has Slown My Brain

Here I sit hoping to write
Nothing new it seems under the sun
Perhaps God now and love
What I need is the fairer sex
That would be nice
I've done my penance




Diary

I am not a poet
But this is some sort of diary
Thoughts you want to keep
Others to exorcize
The bible says that the curses in it
Will be bestowed upon those who wish
To lengthen it.

## Newness of The New Day Sun

I shall awake and open my eyes
I look around
A new day has begun
I will pray in thanks for the new day
I will pray for all those around
The newness of the newday sun
And hopes for everfull fun
The newness of the newday sun
Poetry perhaps
Testament perhaps
Love for the blessings bestowed upon me
Pray for those less fortunate
Pray for everyone
What wisdom lays in proverbs
I can't decide what is the best of the bible?
My faith on uncertain grounds
My love on uncertain grounds
I love my family
You love yours
Hope that you can
Hope for'man'
Kindness for women
Kindness for clan
The newness of the newday sun
What is new?
Nothing new under the sun?
Beyond perhaps

The newness of the newday sun
Permutations
Cosmic vibration
The universal wave function
And a theory of everything


Love

Dare I visit love?
Dare I enquire? About love?
A treatise a volume
Expansive everlasting
Yet within?

Dare I visit love?
Will love visit me
Everywhere and infinity
Eternity?
Expansive everlasting

To what use is an
Education put?
Love for humanity
And not just the taste
Higher beings eat
And our love replace.

Visited upon the gods
Visited upon the shods

Love and creation
What is love?
A feeling reciprocated
Indefiniated never vacated
Except when she leaves
Her virtue at the door
Her hope for another more
His hope for another more
Can god be the only object of love?
Can a creation be the only object of god?
Visited by love visited by greed
Visited by sexual need.


Author Author Author

Dare I to dream?
Dare I?
Care converses
Care subversive
Fair in shameness
Fair in blameless
Stare to the vastness
Stare to crassness
The miny man
The shiny tan
E glassy eyes stare
Author, author, author
am I there?

A place a name
Community , destained
How shall I learn
Oxygene reaffirm
Replace confirm
Friendship develops
Hope envelops
To make incandescent
The cold barren shores
But only seasonally
The cold has a place
The bubbles the fizz a race
Up into a blanket of stars
Up into the newday afars
To bring closer the daunting love
To real, appreciate the intrigue
As you wheel in your forfeit
And devilness conceal
To replace the class, the flash
Of all we dream in subverted soup, we cream.


The Limiting Page

I play with the material
Of what I do not know
These blue lines pull my pen to order
My furtherance from disorder?
Perhaps a revealing of the covered

Neuronet creating  intentions
Creating my mind my brain
Math math math
To reveal determined, freedoms block
Pull my words together
This pen is empty


Those Devils

Is all hope for my parents gone
Have those devils stole a happy retirement?
To withdraw in poverty and sickness?
Or can we turn this adversity into good.
In a capatalisk sysktem 'we reject'
Your bid for justice of your work
By their fruits you shall know them.
The good that comes from believing
In the goodness of mankind
The goodness of fair handed justice
To give what one is deserved of
To party the sad times with
Everflow beings to give light
And hope.those devils
Is it just misunderstanding
Or the plot the greed bought off
For there deeds?

Alone &…

No longer alone
Just at home
Sitting in my room
Thinking of doom

I hope for security
Bless me with surety
The birds chirp
The muse it leads
To more music deeds
The end of the tape
Batman has a cape
And superman curls.


The Absurd

I sit here listening, thinking
Thinking of life
About life is there meaning
The vastness of infinity
The depths of despair
The heights of creation
Lost bread for nations
Picking up from the sounding
Jarred and chronologie
Time A series, B series
Relative time?

I believe in eternity
I believe in absolute time
I think
Hopefully I rhyme.


 Love Nature

How many meanings of the word Nature?
What is the best sense to keep
Growth of foliage
Pristine lake? Crystal Sea?
To ride a whale watch tour boat
To sit next to clear cold clean
Reaches to the deep
A sanctuary to enjoy
They are everywhere. live with your creations
Live by good deeds, oxygene comes
From grass and weeds
A transition. the wavelength not seen
To sight intellectual eyes the mind
Let's make it all all right.
Things and symptoms
Signs and compact cars
I choose words
I choose
I choose life I choose nature
I choose technology
This poem is techne'
This is reaching discovering

I share to myself
God shares to me
Keep your hope your light
Fade away burn away
Walk away
Live by nature from the fight.
Art in this next line
Love in my sights
The flows and balances
Energy converges and dissipates
Universe oscillates.


Home

Here I've looked again
Do I love you, did I love you?
No, but why cry at that
To be forgiven the strength to be
To be good, as the time passes
To stay good, to make a stand
God takes task with us
When we've slipped
Minervas owl is scarred
The days pass and we learn
To learn yet to regress
To end with the best
Is good boring?
Is that why I slip so much?

To give thanks.
That would be a plus
The past is the past
Let thy will be done.


Nanomorality

All there is-nothing
A swirling abyss-absence
A kernel kisses the sky-supernova erupts
Nanotechnology-ant computers
Nothing absence, supernova erupts to ant computers
Freedom evolves
Fate locates
Universes within universes it seems
Everything seems big
When you make yourself small
Madness denied
Love forgotten
Yet love sleeps next to you
The morning hopes and prays
The fires of destruction quenched
The lights of cities
Shared in justice
Yet energy flows from expectation
Yearning, searching, enveloping
Care, forgiveness, precision
Precision in care

Giving just the right amount
Taking a just share
Any shares left
Some for everyone
Helping hands
Sonorous mountains
Echoes through healthy trees
Sifting sands from pouring brooks
Into the sea
The sea
The hope, the salt
Of the earth


Conservation

So I write on dead trees on the other side
The soul of airs giving cares
The ink of my pen a friend and riches
Seldom seen, to travel the earth
Helping in kind to be judged, critiqued
A soul unfurled, unwravelled
And royalty learns, science proper
Pseudo-Popper (pauper) Kuhn
Like the Wittgenstein, Popper clash
The Kuhn Popper clash, the next bought book
To capture to bracket, what is an intentional
Stance, listening pointing, fearing.
Conservation of memes, genes, clear

Breathing, clear thinking freeing
Grasping, gasping, fastening my little intent
In a big ocean are great octipii
Great squid and super leviathans
Yet a universe, I'm so small, it's so big
Yet I'm so big, its so small, lots of small
Lots to fall, lots to rise, I surmise
My death will be felt by those I love
To have to face my loved ones death, not all
So I hope, will God give me what I need
Or what I want, language envelope
Hope develops, space permeates and
Time…time is a minstral in the
Galley the gallery, singing our eats
Our slurps vocal vulgar burps
So now I'm a man, I don't embrace
A feminine side do I have one
Pansy artist what calls, were you
Made that way? Or can you fight your genes
Fight your memes?


Hell

Do not take me there
I need no cold blistered throne
The source of the 'albedo's' pain
Is in the depths of perdition
And the throne is never there

The devils done me wrong like always
Or is the good still there
God and the Devil some sort of plan?
The souls into man
The depth of silent hearth
The space tight wrath.
And writing to revamp our morality
And we're left a casualty?
Perhaps I should have listened to the others say
The devil is bad turn to god
But how could any Christian turn back
From a being in need
But played the fool I wagered
On what I believed
And now I know not what it was
That I needed
The music is my gateway to heaven
Is hell just code for Hellas
And the ancient Greeks
Is life about more than weeks
Stupid rhymes come all the time
But there comes a feeling
When a poet is spieling.


This New Trip

Where by all the Gods shall I go?
Now I wander to be like the father

And new eruptions bring a swinging spring winter
All reverse the truth-those poets
All reverse the time but we are clear on
All on the horizon of love
Full merits into forever wonder serve
But bull giants rode tall measures
Meaning inject I have lost my mind

Vangelis

Some say I was a madman
I was just a madman
Some say she was a sad maam
She had no master plan
Some say I could be a glad man
But no fear for Saturn
No fear for envies burn
No fear for any return
Staring at the past
What any date may signify
So long ago, so clear
So hurtfully endeared, endeared
So long ago, so clear
And feeling God
What would Heidegger say?
So alone, always alone
Never together when I listen to music
Me and God such distance
And early reflection

Lifes constant resurrection


Life Out Of Balance

A life out of balance
Not an original idea
Not a single grace
Not a single identity
Will I live in transcendens
Will I live with hope
That the future will bring
Or my criticism embraces
Bears me to goodness
What the children hear
My words as of late
Do not destroy
Ever
What you cannot create.

I must peer into eternity
I must see beyond infinity
I must come to grasp with that
Which cannot be found
Witch chanting the sound
I must come to compare
Somewhere with everywhere
I must find the hidden
Secret holy truth

The blood of my body
The water I carry
And the brain
That was lost in the loop
Madness and sanity
It breathes and devours
Takes the last stand
The the one for the home stretch.


Journal Entry

Staring at the faithless up
Believing just long enough
But not enough
Journal entry
Action packed disaster
My life will become
I have tasted hate
Its bitter embrace


As Above So Below 2

"I will fly to the other side"
To all of you I will not confide
My secrets to eternity outside
Of outside
Outside of inside
I will never die

I will implant in your brains
My code my essence
To reemerge with consciousness
In a body of choice
With memory and eternal love
To the one I choose
You won't wrest it from me
I am back to live
That I cannot forgive
Never ever forever
As above so below
The furies in my blood
Apeiron, fire on
No word for me no covering law
You have lost all I am
I am stronger now
I am wiser now
I cannot play the game
And you you're a shame.


See You In Hell

I'll drag down the very last
The last soul
Reserve a home for my son
In heaven
You will feel my torture
You will know my pain

Will you ever be the same?
Rotting and burning
Feeling seeing knowing
"there's nothing you can say
To make me feel worse
Than I do
I guess that I'll see you
In hell"
Hell is just the beginning
Further further dwell
Evil is pure forever
The pain I feel the truth
What you did to me
I will transcend.
Eclipse.


Lineage

A line so pure
Hallowed be fire
Passing on through
All eternity
Apeiron the circling mysts
Magic is just the beginning
The very beginning
Using my words to get at me
Can you see
Can you feel

What you did to me?


Time to Think

Thinking on this page
Inscription
Encryption
No free restrained fiction
To last to overcome
Privation
Devastation
Spelling nation
Thinking on this page
Time to write
Writing nothing
Its sonic embraces
Casual displaces
Soul aware at birth
Removing impediments
Spelling nation
Love, light, hope
Eternal truths
Relative youths


Monsters

Todays children assailed by

Superheros, monsters, creatures
Bad guys we hit and destroy
Win on a cartoon reason
The season and music envelops
Thesaurus develops
Spelling nation
Monsters start to bite
Without rations
Biting, crewing, clawing and chewing


Inner Journey

To pull from the inside revealing lines
Pulling outward, outward from single lined times
The length of the poem coincides outwade in the water
God improves sets to the divine challenge
Is this where hope lies connected to the mind?

Another length and the free flow of words
An f singles out in the winding rhymes
Don't force your style the word and voice sounds
I'll measure you your share of the profound
Sad for God? Or sad for me
My loved ones loved ones
Heaven is the hope please.

Have I grown and learned?
Or will I for my sins burn
Will I just dissipate in the ground

And my soul die without a sound?
Let me see to love you all
Solipsism is it Gods downfall
Feel for God for his truth
Feel forever feet and boots
Feet and boots life and shelter
Perhaps we're boots
Boots on Gods immense toes
Or maybe more to grow
Pray for God pray for the poor
The disillusioned the lonely boor
Out on the misty moors.


One Two Three Four

Is the universe finite?
I would like to know
God is everything
Not wholly other
Lonely, rage against
Give life, feelings and memory
Future prosperity
Maybe enough would be to
Feel like a human
Do you feel like a human?
Can we know any other?
Questions contain something
Of the answer

Was Plato right
Has the form blessed?
Tippler says 'no vital force'
Just a physical body
But the omega point
Seems everybody is thinking
Of the end point.


God

Do I wish to know you better?
This paper your gift
Your creation
To know your mysteries
To know your hope
I drink
The feeling calls
Must be a sin
Or so is said
A glimpse of pleasure
Does reason provide
The schism of love
To pull apart
To think again
What is my purpose
Many thinks need mending
What's a thing?
Hope depending

I listen to yes
To see language
Pour upon the page
Friends gone
Not forgotten
The love can pull together
Much to be seen in heaven
Hope and love
Do I move on
Find another the one
To miss my son
Your power
Your majesty
Of the planets
The universe
Instantaneous creation
I'm so little.


Words and Thoughts

Bless the children
The mommies the daddies
Bringing hope to us
Love to us
Light and strength to us
Don't recede into the dark
Metaphor displace
Benevolence replace

More benevolence
Freedom in the flow
Spending words collect them back
To redistribute wisdom
Liking to reason
Liking the new season
Love, hope, faith believing
Edify, classify do not destroy
Connect feel and allow
Gods love to act by you
This is the neatest I have written
For a poem
From my home to yours


## The Practice

Hope lasts, love lasts, art lasts, science lasts
Paradigms shift matter evolves
God is the truth a believed one
Death is a practice
Life is a beginning
Or can god just not be proven
Pure act pure potential
The universe the middle


## The State of Exception

Here is what I feel

I try to think the limit
And I am reduced
I try to think the beginning
But I am only practicing death
Spelling nation
The camp it prys open
All our good feelings
It reduces us to bare life
Born to suffer
The refuges flee tyranny
But then they find the camp
So camps a sheltering
Some camps
To think the limit
Infinity calls
A threshold of hope
A mind transferred
As a program
To escape the matter


Nazi

The devil may care
God does
What we have allowed
To take place
Left our hope at the door
The violence destroying

The pure eternal return
Progress attempts to better
Those evil days
Leave polemics now.


Feeling

I am sitting here
And feeling is slipping
Just feeling God
The joy of mechanical madness
The sound of Philip Glass
Not quite brilliant
Just the wreckage
But of the promised land
Am I here?


Corporation

What is the worth of free thought?
What is the worth of a poets words?
Can the words of evil be redeemed?
Made good to give wisdom and hope?
Can the evil deeds of a person be forgiven?
Can a man be better than his past
To bring his guilt to hope?

His hate to love?


## Ossification

At the tender age of 31
You will be cemented materially
In your ways

Your bones turn solid
Like your arteries and brain

All the body people have learned
How to trap the soul
To be trapped is my destiny

I cannot say 'it' anymore
It evolves and grasps new technology

The whos and whats of phenomenology


## Dance of the Requiem

Dancing are we all towards
A final funeral
Learn to write
Back to print
To the wind
Let beings be it seems

Almost cacophony
But pleasantly
Art is a respect
A thankful thanking
To make the beautiful
Worlds back to world
One love in all eyes
Different loves in one, Eye
The other red shade brain
Transfers to the other side
Dance of the requiem
For Mozart all marching
It seems all art opens
A time for itself
Looking up at love
What was lost and what
Will be gained
Watching or waiting?
Nature

Natures place
Mans place
Where does person go
After all the revolutions
Any homes left at all
Always wandering

Nature is crying
Holding out the once

Bountiful hands
Here my writing
Compromises
Ink and paper

Regeneration
Recontemplation
Live livers
Life givers
Hopeful taking
Hopeful accepting

Save save
Do not spend
Become one
With the hope
let it become
your dope.


Life Dance

Prance prance  prickly bastardly
Science like soundly patiently
Flow meters computer beaters
Winners on the prowl, the walk
Mimicking soundly
Science like beratingly
Pulsing vision arcane potions
magic patiently

Dance dance wherever-you maybe
You may be, becoming became
Hate seethes in every inch of me
Hate brutal hate
Yet upon reading this methodically
They will hate –perturbedly
Not knowing why they hate more
They call it the good
To stamp out irradicate
Confiscate manipulate
To judge-enh!
Enh enh enh!
Fuck me take me
Distribute me
Lie to me
To see passively
I sleep
I sleep into
Some horrifying myst.
Mist-missed
Hit-annihilated
Killed- if you could
Would you?


To Praise The Songs of Kate Bush

One thirty five in the night-the mourning
At having lost lady corporeal

On to the recorded bat lady angel
Singing those eternal songs
Genius talent, soliciting
My donation again in mentioning
The music, the wide world
Don't believe the global village propaganda
It is still wide deep and beautiful
Like her sonorous music.


Schizophrenia

Hi I'm a schizophrenic
I'm not an alcoholic
I'm afraid the drinking
Would drive me crazy.


Jacobs Ladder

To heaven
To any place
Or is that the point
To hell
To hell.


Of Great Men and Women

All of us come from the great mind

Of God
My little entrapment's here
Tell only of my fear
That I have not been molded
From that great intellect
Perhaps my last regret
I did not value the gifts I was given
The good for what we have striven
In time of conflict defer to love
If you have been broken been deceived
Here is a little reprieve
Descartes talks of the universe
And I of those born to hell
That each of us are part
Of that great creation
Perhaps life is only the beginning
Of what we are made for

And at the end of the song
Martyrs devils and angels
Tragedy knocks at the door
Triumph believe in what you are
A good encapsulated
Potentiality believe become
Do not be deceived
But beware my poetry
Is not clear distinct
Not complete
You must judge to compete

But love to care…


## Apeiron

The nation stands in awe
A requiem of sorts
Stands NASA abreast
Beyond after
Look my seekers
My yearners
Arts cause
Beyond afar
Yea seekers
Joggers on the nile
Words come and dwell
Come oh yea afar
Yea afar


## Things to Eat

I sit here full
Drink in my belly
And food too
Thinking of the rocky universe
How could food become?
Available to eat, something good
From the indifferent

# M

M is her name
Returning from Russia
She sits in front of the store
Pink hair and smiles
Encouraging me to do my masters
Am I smart enough?
Or lazy, uninterested
I thought she was uninterested
But asks will I be at the store
Tomorrow, tomorrow she may invite me
To be her companion friend
A very beautiful girl, I like the way
She dresses
Does she just like to tease
Or is that her femininity
Pray for me so that I can love
Again.
Night sprite


# Words Return

In the beginning there was God
And he was with the word
The word was eclipsed with madness
And humanity relapsed
Into a prior state

Jesus built the universe
The word was used to welcome
Being became friends with things
Things were beings
Man and humanity the tool maker
Friends with Gods
Yet to die
To face other tomorrows


Solitude or Loneliness?

That voice that claims it is a self
What can you build to put on my shelf
A sculpture an heritage of sorts
Should we find friends, play sports

I sit here listening to a foreign opera
Me? Never I was never raised that way
To be society but here I am
Creating culture
Vultures circle to reduce and cover
Everyone needs a cover for their entente
Retreat repeat colour fonts
Enable a table to lay upon
Your books your wallets
And hopes madness.

Still some measure will do to find
Hope and class dignity reduce the crass

Obnoxious young boys will grow will learn
If anyone can teach.
So reach and grab the words
To break your loneliness
Solitude is healthy
Loneliness is wealthy, with pain
And down the drain
How simply insane!


## Entente

To agree on our loneliness in an ocean
Of despair. To read, to write, to speak
To give resonance of hopes, singular hope
For everyone together all the weather.


## At Having Lost a Love

Now to look back at what I miss
The misty sky ethereal stars and a kiss
A kiss long forgotten lost in previous dreams
I do not long for her face but I see it
I don't have to imagine her looks
Like all the ladys when their mad they bite


## Enfeebled

Enfeebled by the drunken bliss
Missed too much love but a family
Together to survive to stay the misty
Cruise ships from other smaller lands
To visit the shores of discontent
Again together again forever
That was the dream, to wait in line
To reminisce at many previous years
Looking back into the fuzzy past
To seek to believe to comfort
Your God, my gods, my God
What have I done, left love by the side
Of a ship in Sargasso seas
Future now future previous
Become into forever become
One with the hope


Words

Neatly written to convey characteristics
Half genius to anyone who calls
Music becoming planets of war
Conveyance (spelling) distinctly on

Neatly written to convey characteristics
Flute, clarinettes (spelling) cellos.
Meaning constructed

Neatly written to offset ballistics
A computer for writing on
Why the greed for power?
The flows of soul bearers
God!


Heideggers Death

Faith leaving, faith believing
Sober approachment and the neurons
The neurons characterizing enveloping
The brain in recidivism, cleavage
Bosons, bosums, antartica
To say something new
To demonstrate an understanding
Of meaning, of grasping the leaving!
I am not able to judge the past
Or am I, answer in words
Sounds, and listening to the sober
Resonance graspind tho philkoskovy
To pull in the vulgar leaving trees
An important relapses
Ordinary madness?


El Greco

Techne-ontos-arete
Nous-logos-phronimos

To think the limit
To cross the Rubicon
To spend thriftly
To justice and economics
Ordering a household on what is learnt
The balance, a betraying
And a dangerous game.
The energy permeates the spoken limbs
Extending pushing pulling pulsating
Vibrating, exonerating captivating
To captivate my body with energos
To capitulate at the remembrance
To hear to listen to understand
To pollute society with unwise unrepentant
Words
To help, the hands of kindness
To see the treasure in other lands
Forgiving, investing, listening, learning
The gravity of resonance.


What You Do Anyway

It's what you do anyway
That matters
The sky the stars
Infinite pebbled beaches
What you do anyway
How you love

How you play


Gods Vessels

Today I awaken
Look upward
To see the great expanse
Today I will believe upward
To think
To create
To be the hands of divinity
I hope I will be chosen
To take some credit
Yet all
Inalienable rights
Maybe it's just me
And my biology
And the ever reaching
Advancing infinity


Power

The power of love awaits-withdraws, leaves
Do I love the girl, did I love the girl?
A man who crys is not a man something says
The fear of designated, social gender
An asexual "shell of a man preserved"
A single age a lifetime enough for her?

Could I live my life, with one person who I
Did not want to spend eternity with
Can something absolute be reduced to relative love?
So I say to you my kind benefactor
Who looks upon the case presented, my life
I love her like the others all were worthy, perhaps
God gives what we need not what we want?
The question, hovering, displaying the other
Is the other God? Solipsism reappears
Faith hope love. If I turn to these ideas
These possible fictions then what is not real?
Unfair. Human questions human hopes, the superman
The value of hope is cross species
The hope of peanuts on a patio
The blue jay cries to his fellows
'come here my comrades peanuts!'
Perhaps these were my previous loves-peanuts.
'I shall share these with my comrades'
But love will someday be deliciously mine.


Next To Nothing Lays the Prayer

Can you take me through dark days
Will hope prove in multifarious ways
Can credence, essence, bodily memes
Betray?
Bodily memes? Chemicals, energy focus
Levels of flows, scoping beyond

Wilting trees yet robust within
To last the camera eyes to pull
The records of sin from foreign imprints
Matters for travelling, to meet
Fuelling hopeless fires, power
Power to feel to give to know
The human kind, physician heal
Doctor kneel, to your gifts, give
Spreading latent through spiders webs
Music sounds, your head, your ears
Telephone ' I have seen a speeder'
So why can cars go faster
The measure for pleasure?
Or power when stepping outside
Inclusive exclusion, exclusive inclusion
My life now bare, you will be killed
You will be excluded, the field you
Invested has folded, we are memes in
Your mind, we protect our own kind
Incomplete measures alive?
Pray or feel, exclude
Or interest in one
Many Gouldian interviews
Overlooking the process
Cultured or butchered madness
And prayer to be better
To hold the template to the letter.

A Writers Request

I am requesting I am waiting I am praying
Reacting to the music I hear
The love, the care, the hope
The universe, universes, being, immanence
At not believing an end to my I
I am requesting I am waiting I am praying
Peeing when I have to
To thank for words for being a witness
To love creation, to love shuffling
Shuffling cards in a monstrous deck
A beach, bespectacled pebbles
The clean clear water washing the trip
Drip drip the power of existence to my lap
I must write to remind if I dare
The poor are they everywhere, will they
Be with us always. A reminder to value, to
Treasure our freedom
I am requesting I am waiting I am praying
To be a better person, yet sex, yet eros
A craving? A positive reinforcement matrix
To pass on the genes? Or romance with
Beauty, when you look it in the eye
She looks back with a smile.
But you see I am not the real thing
A writer is genius I am uncle Remus
Stink foot!

Delius

I never thought I could Bleed
Like I bleed
But I have chocolate here
And music
What voice can I give to the faceless many
Suffering, toiling, dieing
Yet I will die
Dead in the grave
To the soil, to the bugs
Survival for days
"ta ta ta hmm"
"ta ta ta"


Always Alone?

So I walked a million miles
A million Rome's fight
A million thrones
The bight
To hide away, to write
Where is she will she ever come?
Do I look or wait
Some say to look is all you can do
But you find when you don't look
She's out there somewhere

Headache

What you do anyway, the miracle of words
Complete and utter war uttering pease
Pease pudding, peace on a good footing
Is peace secured by preparation of war?
Ordinary madness, the phronemos must declare
Do not waste your time here
Headaches and other pains
Today I awaken and look to the hidden
Stars sights, meanings and a journal
Of competence, competing and words
Playing on repeating.


The Fallen

Some gave most, if a soul
Some gave all, if then no
My son their daughters and sons
Is there an answer is there comfort
To leave hope if it means madness
To leave only jesting sadness?
S A D N E S S
At the loss we all share
A world community
A galaxy community
A universe of scales and justice
Eternal outside yet immanent

Justice for the fallen
The given
The striven
And shortness of breath
The spirit in and out
And aunts and uncles.


Circle

Standing in the circle
Will you thrust your sword
Into the ground?
What lies in wait outside?
Humanity a primitive species
Or perhaps nothing
In wait and watching
You must realize that you
Have much power have
Because you must try because
See the three, the six
The ancient river stix
To be protected how so?
Don't you know?

The second round
Doomed to the sea
Shark infested waters
An oil slick follows you

Swimming the sea
A dagger in hand
A luminous spheroid
Rises out of the swelling seas
Shines a light on you
Standing in a circle.

The last effort to stop
The necronomicon
To release or unleash
A no future
A no brainer
If words can be laws
And formulae what words
Need the circle?


How I Have Sinned

In a lifetime there are many
Sins piling on top of each
Every hellish desire
Becoming out of reach
Living into the past
The pain of history
The second sight
The spent time of the night
Everywhere and everyone
I eat, I eat, I sleep

My sin, everywhere
When I die the universe
All around and the sound
The spinning spheres
All those bitter years.


## The Sound of Madness

The sound of holy God
The mother father embryo
The time spent
The utter long time
The spinning years
Leaping awash
The scaling heights
Remember


## The Loard

I am the deaf
I cannot hear you
I am the blind
I cannot see you
I am the poor
I cannot buy you
Can you save me
I must save myself
I must lift my load

My heavy cross
I cannot tell you
A heavenly gate and castle
Must we live with death
Must we live with life
I want the honest court
The severe middle
The lightest load
I die in despair
Loathing in tragedy
 Afear awash
Ashore
Wrecked
I burn again
On the coals
But I am walking
I am living
I get stronger
Stigmata
The loard


Confession

Is judgement day
A human project
Could I have precipitated
The end of all mankind
Perhaps I'm insane

Perhaps simply misguided
Could I have sold my soul
For free
So all the souls could leave hell
Could I take my soul back
And send them into inferno
I am not God
But thought I could be
As a god
To manipulate
And program many minds
Confrontation became real
To work existence
To make the world deliver
The medication stops the
Confrontation
My unconscious subliminal mind
Does the work now
But am I in a chemical
Straightjacket
Will life deliver
Maybe I could go to church
Study ethics
History presents the problem
War and concurring
Should I reject all hope
For an afterlife
Clearly questions
Clearly no answers

Gravity Well Travellers

I stare at your deep oceans on high
Around your rocky coasts the grass it clings
I have travelled the aeons across femto planets
Wells of progress and regress breathing in and out
That is your land in my eyes
Surrounded by air and sea
What To Leave

Goodbye questions
Goodbye all care
Everywhere
The blue tinted chrome
The shiny epidome
Circular ruins
In timeless expanse
Space applied
Time as well
Becoming future
Whens and thens


Fire Garden

Burn burn troubling to churn
Out of smoky flaming dens
Creature comforts plumes

Fumes and more toxic ruins
All the love that was
Could be burned
Save every piece you can
Do no longer waste
Consuming reducing
All good to ashes
Did we not learn our lesson
From those fighting legions
World war worlds embittered
Bring your hope to light
To bear
So we may all live in luscious
Thick green gardens

Where's My Genius?

On the beach?
Foreign lands?
Books, paintings, drawings?
Sound?
Love and hope?
Parenting and work?
Poem?
?
???...


We Are Them

Who are they?
What from what on?
Build it, they will come
Peace, peace must be
Together we hope, we work
To make things better
To bring hope, love, life
To an embattled collective
A dissidents soul in freedom
Carrying the message
The text of revolutions
Need not, not now
Food behind the ideologies
Please don't look
Don't sever the heads
Of brilliance, the screams
Of terror in the night
Don't sever love of god
Don't sever humanity from love
Lend a helping hand
We are them, they are us
'if you only knew' they say
I know and I say
These principles, we are them
On through a dark night
To a concrete oasis
The machines, say nature
Say mothers of prosperity
Save the trees this paradise

A hell for so many
Do our computers bring the hope
Or subjection, link the needs
Supply the needs, love in light.


Love Makes Him Glad

Of what purpose is a writer?
This writer
Any writer
In the winter of our discontent
The winder of our malevolence
To live for benevolence
To spell seek and bring back
To organic the cities
To plant the trees of hope
The trees of life
The children must know
What it is like to run in the woods
To feel a part of nature
To taste some of its treasures
My son needs to know love
A universe so seemingly cold
To change a flat in 30 below
A winter war
A hearth in summer
Bones of many bodies
Books of many karates

Discipline to train the soul
To bring provohito in altum
Fishy waters, fishy waters
Surrounded by power everywhere
Some say he was a madman
But love makes him glad.


The Stars

Suns and seemingly infinite
Scoping and yearning in awe
Expanse never ending
Yet the moral law within
Forever and ever
Can you hear it?
Can you hear it?
Infinity eternity sublimity?
Can you feel it?
Revolving spinning vortex
Seas and soups
Spinning into time
Spinning out of time
Mars on the horizon
Horizons on the horizon
Power, love hope awe
Fear, terror, signs and signals
The signified
Symbols and efforts

The stars, the sky, the beyond!


## Is That My Duty?

So now I am free again
Has my heart mended?
Shall I find true love again?
Will I stick with it?
Listening again to the sounds of anxiety
To turn fear and slipping time back
To better years
Have I time for anyone but my son?
For myself I guess.
I can no longer feel joy
Happiness is some sort of ego state
A funny show a funny movie
Still moves me but
I feel a hollow shell
A hollow wreck of life
Still I am lucky
I want to do what is right
I want the world a better place
Peace of mind a chimera
To see joy in anything
Happiness is doing anything but sleep
My dreams don't stick to memory
And my back is going
Headaches and groin aches

Looking for love
But I must remember God
God is now in my mind
I must seek grace and hope
There is complete beauty
Everywhere in nature, a spring walk
A spring sunshine and a warm breeze
Winter no longer total discontent
I want genius but is that my duty?


Vacuum

Each drink-closer to death
Each sunrise draws the breath
Ideas swarm the naked mind
Ideas torn the grassy knolls find
A woman in my dreams calls
Yet I can't remember her face as it falls
the curtain the sale de bain pours
Over the cliffs of recompense
Sardonic toils and embraces

Each star far above beyond
Each duck, trees surround a pond
Ideas of destruction the end
Ideas of nuclear hope try to mend
A rhyme at the beginning
A hope we like spinning

They call from up above
But yet below turns a dove
Right to write to find
Keep trying keep flying

A vacuum suck the neurons out
A computer fills the cavity, the soul departs
Or does it stay to witness evolution
The change from the old life to the new life
A vacuum sucks the stars together
Motion hurls them apart
They are coming it has been said
They are coming will we be dead?
The philosophers what is it they do
Think, project, build, control, uncover
Help, ignore, combine, create
Disclose, where shall we find ourselves
This time.


Invasion

They are coming from deep outer space
Our computers must be controlled
They come for peace to help us
Is this true? I ask my God
I look through my telescope to the stars
Where from where with how could they come?
Older parts of the universe I say

But does that shock you?
Perhaps they're here enslaving all the humans
A philosophical book on invasion
The mind controlled the soul trapped
The energies withdrawn


Flowers

A walk in a beautiful garden
The purple shards snake off the trees
The water trickles from the brook onto
A dead carcass landing in your eye
A bird in the eye jucky jucky!
A hope that this is not my park
But the rows of roses their beautiful smell
Can I hope in words to match this
No but the drama yea man the drama
Crazy I to five beyond the bee hive.


The Vastness of Space II

Do I know you space?
The universe is greater than we can know
Can I bracket it?
Is there any meaning here?
Or just a feeling
Feelings are meanings of a sort

The freedom of language might permit
Do I dare speak?
Of that I do not know?
Having come into contact
Snowy peaks the costly embrace
To peer out of land based scopes
Does the object know it is watched
Triangulating the moment for place
Thought, time, love
Gravities of attractions
Beings outside your windows
Empty plates, food embraces
The full stomach, the burning bush
Talking, giving thought
Directions, goals
People say in the sea
They glance upwards some inwards
And wisdom comes with the dawn
The light re-envelopes, gives breath
The vastness of space
Outer space inner space
Mega pixels, nano pixels
Femto pixels, little particles
Fly computers, virus junkies
The drugs of scale
To feel the fly, to see the sky
And forever hold the real.

The Clocks of Time (The Vastness Of Space III)

All of us connected the heart pulls
To call the silence up from the depth
To make action, to produce, to distribute
All together now, is war a fact of life?

"desperate", "destined", friends to be met
Call from the depths give birth to hope
A wave rolls in from the ocean
Am I smothered at this time

Seal a voice that calls of many
The thought that we must give
Falling into racism but God will answer
Look to heaven, don't let the war dictate

Listening to my words before there
Am I there, so many children?
Why the children?
Am I losing my faith right now?
People must give money, hope, some love
Don't sell your soul
Find the real the real reality
Is it a good one?
Or unbound, unsung, hamstrung
A leg breaks under backs of a load
Maybe there is a way to distribute
To not give into the easy speak

Easy speak attacking the leaders, easy
 Scape goats. We must try but what?
A stick? Can a stick bring order?
Or unleash a whirlwind a desert dune
And the clocks of time just measure
For another to view.


Suspension Of Disbelief

What will I choose to remember?
The guiles glances
Empty stares?
The love or just beings
Frenzy feeding
'Fuck this world
This universe
Let it all go and rot'
My greed all the treasured moments
Inhaled
'Call me gay?'
'fuck you'
All the symbols, signifiers
Madness, signs, symptoms
Yet I choose to care
You don't and it shows
Contradictions, examinations
Outer space the wanderings
Of dark matter

Can the sun alight?
Bowing at the sun
Millions praying
Do I defend my suspension
Of disbelief.
Having to edit
Hateful words
A must
If intention is good
Then don't hate
This world needs love.


This Side of Belief

Any art? My hope
Or just screaming tragedy
All those innocents smiling
Loving
Does hope approach
Of death, desire
Or death decay entropy
Heat dissipation
Slow frozen health?
A hearth must fire in the
Winter to write
A hearth must shelter in the summer night
The bugs the insects

The creepy crawlies creeping
Over my entrusted body
Did I leave or dissipate
Aesthetics, anatomy
Curly, curly wonders
In my cells, any buyers
Any sells
Entrapments
Madness and freedom.
Fishy lakes, dusty hopes
Blizzards for omnipotents
On heightened plates
Upwards onwards outwards


School

My son soon starts real school
I go back in the fall
The withered leaves will embrace my new cast
Out into the fish of truth
Fish of truth call from the surrounding sea
To write on paper to key in my words
Which way environment calls
To stop the negative voice resounding
In my head.


Summer 2002

Resounding echo, trees face the sky
Mountains clamour up the horizon
Sucks them away
Body soaks the heat, mind the night
Pulling the skin taught and endeavour
Keep calling keep calling


Purify

Pray to right the wrongs
Bodies of memories
Follow or get out of the way
Lead or follow
Lead or get out of the way
Get out of the way
Lead
Follow


Winters Girl

Here I write
Here I cry
At the loss of my creation
To be what I want
Love if I believe
Not knowing enough
Perhaps there is only loneliness

In a sea of faces
Each singing in their brains
The dust, the sand, the pebbles
The rust, broken men
Broken man


Some Say a Heart is Broken

To break my heart
To beak my attitude
To love if possible
To care, to see
To feel, to be
Some say I will break your heart
Will I?
I don't know you yet
You don't know me
Can we ever know anything
The sceptic pronounces
The bed the sleep
Believe and awake
The terror of happiness
Out of reach
Forever gone?
The light will shine.


Another Lost

Another found
Loudness sounds
Happiness frown
My alogin
My affect
My selfish wanderings
To give some light
To give some hope
A midnight prayer
To love to stare
My ear my hair
Yea ok yea ok
Disjunction, absolution
Forgiveness.


Performance

Has technology taken away
The human error
Scales at full speed
No performance
Just programs
Yet art?
Permutations
And a new heart.


At The Edge of Freedom

Racing onward into fizzle of the night
Capture omniscience free into flight
Free winds on brazen winged shores
Flying past oceans of contempt and mores

After dawn the ripples talk stupor
The energy spreads into the smoke
Over lands burnt and brawny
Their thick hills and rolling rocks

Spilling again wasting electrophores
Spores and ambivalence rise
Up from the fear of dissolution
Together we build our homes

Something works through me
Amazed at abilities must be god
Or is it myself turned inward
Amazed At the human core

Again the scriptures appear as history
What guidance for today
To look into the green azures bled
The trees rise to blue skys

Purpose and repent

Journey To Love

Ha ha ha

Laughed at the presence
Still much to value
Much to present


Melissa

Who are you?
Russian student
Bare life
And I am called
Why haven't you called?
Will you call?
Why did you take
My number?


Crap Poem

I don't feel like wrighting anything
This building is full up
Nothing to say at all
Or is work the call?
I hate my rhymes
I hate hate some of my times
Some are good full up
Full up son of a bitch
Crap to the top
They look down
Silly humans, silly times

Our planet was wasted like
Yours too


My Son

My son, my son by'
Love im I does eh!
You would too if you had kids
But my project is serious
Should I take myself that way?
To see him grow to expand and spread
Pushing out his word web talks
Just a child testing boundaries
To talk to be listened to
"love is the only answer
Hate is the root of cancer"
"then"


NanoBots

Crawl out, through polysludge plasma!
Breaking peptides and holy molecules
Fixing present to hand in micro!
Will enters and dissipates along the length

The sun comes into view passing the eclipse
And shoppers ready cards to purchase
The flow enters the tube expansion grid

Castaban reacts and enters
Full met the heat resolves the cruz
Cucibles melt the plasma, it jumps
Out into the chimney
Santa clause appears in the mist
Breakdancers spin
Out, out, on, full up!
Starboard, taxonomy, taxidermy!
The shells expand to meet
The matter gravity lapses into blackness
The singularity pull in and recycles
Particles.
Here I look into my computer
The scope out through the hubble
To sea, machines of eternity
Perpetual, mobile spinning
The attraction free flow
Meaning not encompasses, a summoner.
Nanobots are you terror
or peace?


My Pleasures Are Solitary

I am getting Closer, I am seeing
I have seen before, my nows
In dreams the déjà vu builds
A diseased mind?
Or soul outside of time and space

All of time & space, space-time?


Scrying

Into the well I look to find
Many wishes, many treasures
I hope to come across a new philosophy
I hope to find the contents of many minds
Without some innovative measures
I may lapse into a state of entropy


Gifts

Of insight may bring tomorrows
I still see the flows and the medication slows
But does strong and steady win the race?
When death is a blessing who can tell
To see a body mangled in war
Do you end game to save from pain
Do you talk to open the door.
Gifts are a blessing
Who gives what love exchanged
And there's a happy tot.


What Do I Want?

And what do I need?
A pound of hallucinogenic weed?
To see a different way
To feel a different day?
Wisdom calls wisdom withdraws
And all is a park
Kids on their see-saws.


Rocket Science

Where would you go in my lifetime?
Keep meeting, keep seeking
Keep positive
Questioning the pem, the pen
Flowing onwards, outwards
Inwards, entrails
Weirdness, calmness, coldness
My spirit, yours, and a person
From the past, do you remember
All my love displaced
Polypeptides, glucolycogens
Dissipation, absolution
The pen and my madness
Finding a home
Somehow I'm different
Are you together in line?
Standing in line, let the ship

Float without mischief
Misblankets, misendeavours
Devouring happiness
Hope determines
A direction and love
Placed in a metaphor
Corn and peas
Carrots and fleas
Dogs and cats
Birds and rats
Pushing from the left
Pulling on the right
Stretching in the middle
And spelling while
Listening to the fiddle.


Weight

Gasses soups solids, roofs
Rendezvous outside
Innor and/or light
Fantasy and right
Looking upwards in my room
To the plaster ceiling
Could each be a universe a galaxy
Reiling from disgrace
Or celebration at being Gods face
To us below who must realize

The beauty terrifying beauty
Butterflys in your stomach
A field of spectators and you
Must make the moves
The cheers or boos
Practice goodness let
Your sins and hates lapse
Disappear and create
Good work for good souls
For bad souls a respite
Take your evil and your might
Turn to God to save
To replenish to experience
Mystical revelations, meanings
Weight, gravity, circumlocution
Contribution to the great work
Who can little us all.


Suicide

Sadness and loneliness
will it get you
will you kill yourself
to somehow end
to destroy your hope
your life
and in the end
all for nothing

it engulfs you
sucks your soul away
leaves you crying
and hopeless
never to return
to the days of youth
just endings upon endings

to see not truth
to fear all lies
to be deceived
lied to
led away by the ears
left only with tears

and how will they judge you
all isolated
thinking of themselves
at their loss
they cry not for you

for themselves they gather
to the procession
but maybe God
but why cry-why?

Distribute Control

The score is everywhere
The point in writing, hear the voices
Hear them call in the wilderness
To believe to hope to call in self
Pity self, pity why me?
The believing the escaping, the endeavour
To pull and take to spill to spoil
Space especially space
Trust no one trust no one they are sharks
People are takers manipulate the Gods
The Gods have no worries their
Perpetual machines control and distribute
Distribute control.


Thorny Lie

I am grafted to your skin
But the pricks start to tear
What that made me care
Gone to the smoky wind

Staring out over seas of madness
The swells the nodes
The seas of stars
Planets stirring, Solaris

Lost again, no love to navigate
But inside the liquid horror
Sends prickles down my back

Feeds my fire, connected to the sum


Murder

Justified at a fate
So cruel
To go to hell
Is it better to be a murderer
Of yourself
Or of another?
Meditation to fill up
Your body


Biopsy

Biopsychology physye se yay
Say jah yea?
Pulled taught
Micro endeavours
Silence echoing
Deflecting again
To pull the matter out
Out of hand, pieces
Everywhere the courage
The courage to help, to care
To love
Matter everywhere
Silence echoing

Vastness somewhere
Biopsychology
Biopsy just a bit
Pulled out onto the page
For you to examine
Take love
Take care.


Shoot High, Aim Low

As I try to summons faith courage
To go downtown again
To look for someone
To love
Perhaps no sight
Afear from the drink
The night before
Watch the tv. I think the world
Is erupting again
America, Canada's guardian?
All the Islam seems to be hating
USA.
Will the world erupt into war
Some say a state is perpetually at war
Internation state of nature
People by contract choosing union
Poetry plays in my room
Looking for words and hope

Some measure of happiness
To try again I will.

The Machines of Eternity

Out of forever
Crimson skys?
Sea green tea leaves
I look into the cup
To see
The Machines of eternity

I look too soon
The other side
Of my brain
What do I see?
The machines of eternity

I look again
With time to spend
Not a pocket pence
Yet hence things are better
A new woollen sweater
Cold winds make me free
To ride
The machines of eternity


Tortured By Philosophy

Has philosophy been good to me?
Have I been good to it?
Standing above me defiant
Passively here I sit
Somewhere out there
Somewhere without
Somewhere within it all begins
Pride and torture
To think you can think
When all withdraws
Memory convalesces
Maybe I just torture myself
Am I a philosophy
Profound machinery?
Binary and enslaved
Computer conquers all the days


One Day

My goal to finally die
Other major goals defined
To pass into even one
2001 a space odyssey.
Enough to manage?
Enough to conquer?


Just Remember I loved You

You took my love
And threw it to the dust
Took my love for everyday
Lust
Just remember I loved you
With all my might
You left me with night
Woman you did me wrong
Played that game
And you too
Are a crying shame


How Many Can I Pull Out

The poems the deciphered existence
Love in the light
Can you bear I feel goodbyes
Crashing hating sold love
Sold hope.


I Will Deliver

My Son My Love My Hope
Somehow I will deliver
To your hopes your dreams
Your life
I miss you when you are gone

Printed in Great Britain
by Amazon